From Your Friends At **The MAILBOX®**

W9-BGR-129

730 Journal Prompts

Grades 1-3

Two for Every Day of the Year

Editor:
Susan Hohbach Walker

Writers:
Rebecca Brudwick, Lisa Buchholz, Vicki Mockaitis Dabrowka,
Stacie Stone Davis, Heather Godwin, Cynthia Holcomb, Lisa Kelly,
Laura Mihalenko, Mackie Rhodes, Linda Schwab, Valerie Wood Smith

Art Coordinator:
Nick Greenwood

Artists:
Cathy Spangler Bruce, Teresa Davidson, Nick Greenwood,
Clevell Harris, Theresa Lewis, Rob Mayworth,
Barry Slate, Donna K. Teal

Cover Artist:
Nick Greenwood

www.themailbox.com

730 Journal Prompts

Manufactured in the United States

10 9 8 7 6

Table of Contents

730 Journal Prompts

About This Book

This collection of over 730 journal prompts provides two journal prompts for every day of the year. The prompts are based on holiday, seasonal, and general topics so an appropriate selection is always available to match your students' needs.

Reproducible journal covers and a lined writing page reproducible are also included so solutions to all of your journal-writing needs are compiled in this handy resource.

How to Use This Book

Monthly Journal Response Booklets

Have each student create her own monthly journal response booklet. At the beginning of each month, make one copy of the appropriate monthly cover (see pages 100–111) for each student. Then make several copies of the lined writing page reproducible (see page 112) for each student. Stack the lined sheets of paper, place the monthly cover on top, and then staple along the left-hand side to create the booklet. Have each student decorate her cover with markers or crayons.

Guided Daily Journal Writing

Begin each day with an original, fun, thought-provoking journal prompt. Select one of the two prompts to write on the chalkboard, or write both prompts on the board and instruct each student to select the one that interests her the most. If you have access to an overhead projector, a transparency of the prompts will be a timesaver and can be reused year after year. Have students write their journal entries in their monthly journal response booklets. If desired, hold a class discussion of the daily writing topic before students begin writing.

Independent Journal Writing

Add an independent element to your journal-writing program with this idea. Post copies of a month's worth of journal prompts in a center, or display them in a prominent place in your classroom. Every day, challenge each child to select one prompt from the appropriate day to respond to in her monthly journal response booklet.

A
U
G
U
S
T

August 1

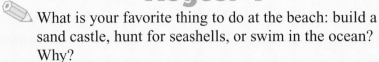

 What is your favorite thing to do at the beach: build a sand castle, hunt for seashells, or swim in the ocean? Why?

 Francis Scott Key, author of the "The Star-Spangled Banner," was born on August 1, 1779. If you could make up a new title for our national anthem, what would it be?

August 2

What is your favorite cool drink in the summer? Explain how to make it.

Would you rather be a tennis player, baseball player, or soccer player? Why?

August 3

 On August 3, 1492, explorer Christopher Columbus set sail with three ships in hopes of finding a new sea route to the Indies. Pretend you are Christopher Columbus. Write a letter to a friend telling about the day you set sail.

If you were given one watermelon seed, what would you do with it?

August 4

 Would you rather be a starfish or a seahorse? Why?

 What are some ways you could earn money this summer? What would you buy with your money?

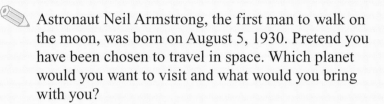

August 5

August is National Inventor's Month! Imagine that you are an inventor and have been asked to invent a new kind of toy. Write the toy's name and describe its features.

Astronaut Neil Armstrong, the first man to walk on the moon, was born on August 5, 1930. Pretend you have been chosen to travel in space. Which planet would you want to visit and what would you bring with you?

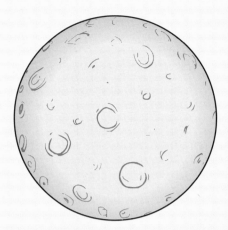

August 6

Write about something you *don't* like doing on a hot summer day. What would you rather be doing?

Write about your last family vacation. What was the most exciting thing that happened?

August 7

August 7 is National Mustard Day! Make a list of all the foods you can think of that you could put mustard on. Put a star by your favorite.

Imagine the temperature outdoors reached 120 degrees. What would you do to stay cool and safe?

MUSTARD

August 8

How do you think the sand dollar got its name?

Describe the clothing you would wear on a hot summer day. Draw a picture of yourself wearing that clothing.

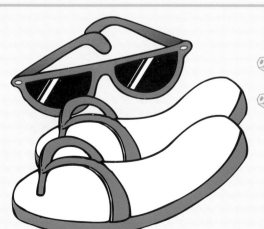

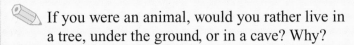

August 9

 Describe something you have done for someone else that you are really proud of.

 If you were an animal, would you rather live in a tree, under the ground, or in a cave? Why?

August 10

 Imagine that your class is getting a pet! What animal would you prefer, and what would your animal live in?

 Imagine that Earth got too crowded and some people had to move to Mars. Describe how going to school on Mars would be different from going to school on Earth.

August 11

 Write a poem titled "Summer."

 If you could make up a new kind of weather, what would it be?

August 12

 List five things you can make from blueberries.

 If you could meet one famous person, whom would you choose? What questions would you ask him or her?

August 13

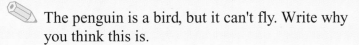

✎ Write a letter to your teacher and persuade him or her to give you an extra recess today. Give reasons why you deserve the recess.

✎ The penguin is a bird, but it can't fly. Write why you think this is.

August 14

✎ If you could invent a new holiday in the month of August, what would it be? How would people celebrate it?

✎ If you could have any fairy-tale character as your friend, whom would you choose? What are some things you would do together?

August 15

✎ While making a sand castle on the beach, you find a bottle washed up on the shore. In the bottle is a message. What does the message say?

✎ You have won a prize to be the teacher in your classroom for a day! What are some things you would teach your students?

August 16

✎ A friend is giving away puppies! Write a letter to convince your parents that you would be a responsible pet owner if they let you have one.

✎ Think of three things you could do today to make someone smile.

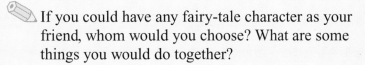
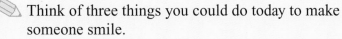

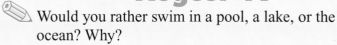

August 17

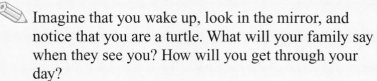

 Would you rather swim in a pool, a lake, or the ocean? Why?

 Imagine that you wake up, look in the mirror, and notice that you are a turtle. What will your family say when they see you? How will you get through your day?

 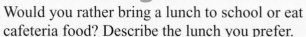

August 18

Pretend you are a caterpillar who is about to change into a beautiful butterfly. Tell about your experience. Describe where you will fly after you've made the change.

Write a note to a friend in class telling that person why he or she is a good friend.

August 19

Would you rather bring a lunch to school or eat cafeteria food? Describe the lunch you prefer.

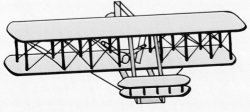

August 19 is National Aviation Day! It is a day to honor Orville Wright, who piloted the first self-powered airplane flight. Why do you think the invention of the airplane was important? How would the world be different if we didn't have airplanes?

August 20

List three things that are taller than you. Now list three things that are shorter than you. Would you rather be taller or shorter than you are now? Why?

Summer will end soon. Make a list of five things you can do to help you remember summer after it ends.

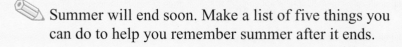

August 21

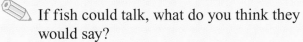 What would you do if you saw trash in your schoolyard or your yard at home?

 If fish could talk, what do you think they would say?

August 22

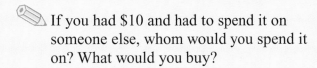 Imagine that you found a treasure chest buried in your yard. What would you hope to find inside when you opened it?

If you had $10 and had to spend it on someone else, whom would you spend it on? What would you buy?

August 23

 Imagine that your mom or dad will be home alone for lunch. In case he or she gets hungry, write the directions for making a peanut butter and jelly sandwich.

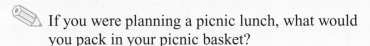 If you were planning a picnic lunch, what would you pack in your picnic basket?

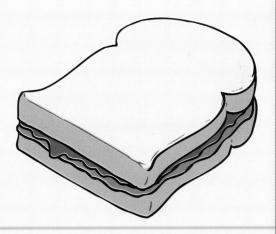

August 24

If you could grow any type of tree in your backyard, what would it be? Why did you choose this kind of tree?

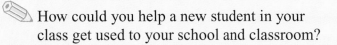 How could you help a new student in your class get used to your school and classroom?

August 25

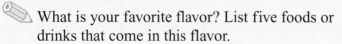

Think of something you could teach someone else to do. Describe how you would teach this.

What is your favorite flavor? List five foods or drinks that come in this flavor.

August 26

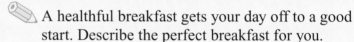

The first baseball game to be shown on TV was broadcast on August 26, 1939. The competing teams were the Cincinnati Reds and the Brooklyn Dodgers. Which position in baseball do you think is the most important? Why?

A healthful breakfast gets your day off to a good start. Describe the perfect breakfast for you.

August 27

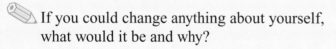

Would you like to go camping in the woods? Why or why not?

If you could change anything about yourself, what would it be and why?

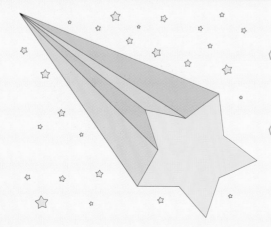

August 28

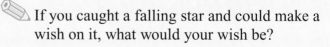

What is your favorite season: spring, winter, summer, or fall? Why? What are some things you do during this season that make it so special?

If you caught a falling star and could make a wish on it, what would your wish be?

August 29

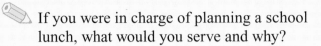

✏️ Write about three activities you can do in the summer that you can't do in the winter.

✏️ If you were in charge of planning a school lunch, what would you serve and why?

August 30

✏️ What are some of the supplies that you think are important to have in school? How do those supplies help you in school?

✏️ What is your favorite movie? Describe your favorite part.

August 31

✏️ If you were given a choice, would you rather ride in a car or a bus to school? Why?

✏️ Write about some good ways to meet new friends on the first day of school.

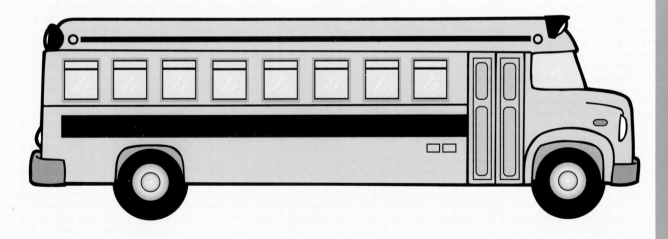

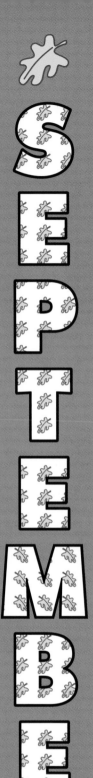

September 1

Write about three things that you saw on your way to school this morning.

Labor Day, the first Monday in September, honors our nation's workers. If you could have any job, what would it be? Why?

September 2

If you were a teacher, what would a day in your classroom be like? Write about it.

September is Ice Cream Month. Did you know that the average American eats 15 quarts of ice cream a year? If you could invent a flavor of ice cream or an ice-cream dessert, what would it be? Write about your tasty new creation.

September 3

Would you rather be an owl or a squirrel? Why?

Imagine that an apple tree could talk. What would it say?

September 4

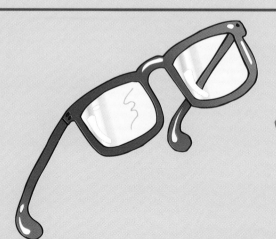

What would you like to learn this school year? How can you work toward your goal?

September is Children's Eye Health and Safety Month. Why is it important to keep your eyes safe? Write a list of eye safety tips.

September 5

 What does the saying, "An apple a day keeps the doctor away," mean to you?

 What can you do to make sure you will have a great school year?

September 6

 National Grandparents Day is the first Sunday after Labor Day. If you could design a hat for one of your grandparents that would show what he or she likes, what would it look like?

 Think about the first day of school this year. What was the best thing about that day? What was the worst?

September 7

 Write about something important that you learned from a grandparent or another special adult.

 Describe three ways to make new friends.

September 8

 Poet Jack Prelutsky was born on September 8, 1940. Mr. Prelutsky wrote a poem titled "I Should Have Stayed in Bed Today." This poem is about a child who is having a day when everything goes wrong. Tell about a day when nothing seemed to go right. Did anything make you feel better that day?

 Imagine the chalkboard in your classroom could talk. What would it say?

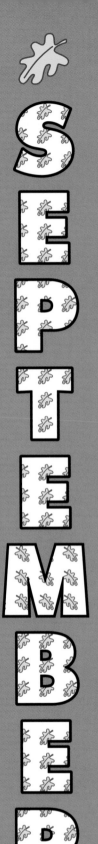

September 9

On September 9, 1850, California became the 31st state of the United States. Why do you think California is called the "Golden State"? If you could give California a different nickname, what would it be?

You are told to pack your backpack to be ready for anything that might happen at school. What will you put in it?

September 10

The second week of September is Substitute Teacher Appreciation Week. What are the most important things a substitute teacher should remember to do?

Football season has begun. Imagine you are a football. How does it feel to go soaring through the air between the goalposts?

September 11

September 11 is 911 Day. When should you call 911? What information should you give when your call is answered?

What would be the perfect school lunch? How would you convince your school board to serve it at your school cafeteria?

September 12

September is Children's Good Manners Month. What are the most important manners to use? Why?

Which do you think is stronger, a rule or a promise? Why?

September 13

On September 13, 1916, children's author Roald Dahl was born. In his book, *Charlie and the Chocolate Factory*, Willy Wonka made extraordinary candies in his factory. If you could create a new fantastic candy of your own, what would it taste like? How would you make it?

The famous chocolate maker, Milton Hershey, was born on September 13, 1857. Describe what makes a great candy bar.

September 14

September 14 marks the anniversary of the start of the first solo balloon flight across the Atlantic Ocean. Where would you like to travel in a hot air balloon?

What do you think your teacher keeps in his or her desk?

September 15

Author and illustrator Tomie de Paola was born on September 15, 1934. His book, *Tom*, is an autobiography. What important events would you include in your autobiography?

Which has the harder job, a school bus or a pencil? Why?

September 16

On September 16, 1620, the Pilgrims set sail for the New World. Pretend you are traveling on their ship, the *Mayflower*. How do you feel about leaving your home and traveling to a new land?

What room would you add to your school that it doesn't already have? Why?

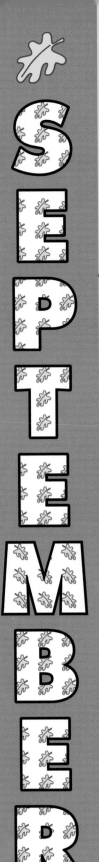

September 17

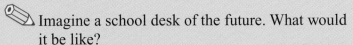

In honor of the signing of the United States Constitution, Citizenship Day is celebrated on September 17. Write about the qualities of a good citizen.

Imagine a school desk of the future. What would it be like?

September 18

To make paper products, millions of trees are cut down each year. How many different ways do you use paper? Describe some ways you could conserve paper.

Pretend you are an apple. Describe how you feel about changing colors as you ripen. Are you proud? Embarrassed? Excited?

September 19

How could you convince the principal that your school needs more playground equipment? What reasons would you give?

Rules help a classroom run smoothly. What would happen if there were no rules in your classroom for one day?

September 20

Design the best lunchbox ever. How would it be decorated? What would be inside?

In the Northern Hemisphere, the first day of fall is approaching. But in the Southern Hemisphere spring is just beginning. Would you rather it be spring or fall? Why?

September 21

✏️ If you were the principal, what would you change about the school?

✏️ What makes a day at school good? Write about a school day that was good for you.

September 22

✏️ On September 22, 1903, the ice-cream cone was born. What makes ice cream such a popular dessert?

✏️ If you invented a homework machine, you would probably be cheered all over the world. Describe how your machine would work.

September 23

✏️ With the start of autumn, we're bound to notice cooler temperatures. What makes you feel cozy when it is chilly outside?

✏️ What are some signs of fall? Use all your senses to describe this season.

September 24

✏️ The last full week in September is National Dog Week. Dogs are known as "man's best friend." If you could pick any animal for a best friend, which one would you choose? Why?

✏️ If you had a dog for a pet, what would you do to care for it?

September 25

✏️ The fourth Sunday in September is National Good Neighbor Day. How can you be a good neighbor?

✏️ Imagine you are a fall leaf. Would you rather cling to the tree or float to the ground? Why?

September 26

✏️ John Chapman, also known as Johnny Appleseed, was born on September 26, 1774. He was famous for planting apple orchards. If you could plant any fruit, which would you choose? Why?

✏️ Imagine you are a worm searching for an apple to eat. Describe the apple you would choose.

September 27

✏️ The last weekend in September is Family Health & Fitness Days USA℠. What activities do you and your family enjoy doing together that would help you get in shape?

✏️ On September 27, 1998, Mark McGwire hit his 70th home run of the season, setting a new world record. What world record would you like to set?

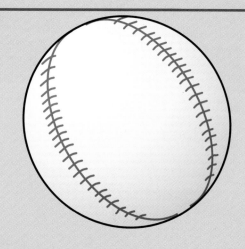

September 28

✏️ You see a new student standing alone on the playground. What will you do?

✏️ Would you rather be a teacher or a principal? Why?

September 29

✎ Fall is a time for animals to prepare for the winter. Some store extra food. Some grow warm fur coats. How do you get ready for winter?

✎ Rank the school playground equipment from your favorite to your least favorite piece. Explain why you ranked the pieces the way you did.

September 30

✎ Write the name of a person sitting near you. Now list at least four nice things about that person.

✎ If you were a fall leaf, what color would you be? Why?

October 1

Today is the first day of October. Write about some of the things you plan to do this month.

Today is the first day of October. Write about some of the things you plan to do this month.

World Vegetarian Day is celebrated on October 1. Describe a meal of only fruits, grains, nuts, and vegetables that you would enjoy eating.

October 2

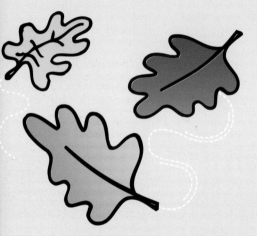

Autumn and *fall* are both names for this season. Words that have the same meaning are called synonyms. List ten more synonym pairs. Now write a story using the words from your list.

It's birthday time for Charlie Brown® and Snoopy®, two lovable comic strip characters by Charles Schulz. Pretend you are invited to their birthday party. Describe the event.

October 3

Fire Prevention Week is in October. You're assigned to create an informational handout to give to people in your community. What would you write to tell them about fire safety?

The five senses are sight, hearing, smell, touch, and taste. What things will your senses experience during the month of October?

October 4

October is National Popcorn Poppin' Month. Think of at least three foods that have the word *pop* in them. List them and write your opinion about each one.

The word *fall* has several different meanings. Write at least two sentences using *fall,* with a different meaning in each one.

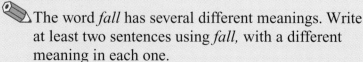

October 5

✏️ How many words can you think of that remind you of October? Write your list on your paper. Now write a tall tale using as many of the words as possible.

✏️ October is National Clock Month. How would your life be different if there were no clocks?

October 6

✏️ The first seven days in October celebrate Universal Children's Week, a time to think about children's needs. What are some things you think all children need to have? List a reason why each is important.

✏️ October is the tenth month. Write about ten nice things you have done this year.

October 7

✏️ Orange pumpkins, orange leaves, orange candy wrappers—the color orange is everywhere in October! Write a paragraph about orange things that you like. Then write another paragraph about orange things you don't like.

✏️ October is National Pasta Month. Pretend your mom or dad does not know what spaghetti is. Write a paragraph describing how it feels, looks, and tastes.

October 8

✏️ Spiders have eight legs. Write a story about a spider's trip to a shoe store.

✏️ The second week in October is National Spinning and Weaving Week. If any creature knows about spinning and weaving it's a spider! Write a diary entry from a spider's point of view describing a day of web weaving.

October 9

✏️ October is Family History Month. Think about a special event that your family was a part of. How will you describe the event to your own children in the future?

✏️ Pumpkins are a tasty treat to eat. Pumpkin pie, roasted pumpkin seeds, and pumpkin bread are just a few of the delicious dishes made from pumpkins! What is your favorite way to eat pumpkin? Why?

October 10

✏️ Don't you just love finishing a meal with a great dessert? Describe the best dessert you have ever eaten.

✏️ Fall means sweater weather. Have you ever lost a sweater or jacket? If so, what did you do to get it back or replace it? If you've never lost a sweater or jacket, write a few tips telling others what you do to keep it from being lost or taken.

October 11

✏️ October is National Stamp Collecting Month. If you could select someone to appear on a new stamp, who would you choose? Why?

✏️ As you pass your neighbor's house, you see the jack-o'-lantern on his front porch change its face from happy to scary. Write a story describing what you think caused this to happen and what your reaction was.

October 12

✏️ The second Monday in October is Columbus Day. It commemorates Columbus' October 12 landing in the New World. Pretend that you are Christopher Columbus writing a letter to the king and queen of Spain. Persuade them to lend you money for your trip.

✏️ If you visit a store this time of year, you're sure to see many masks anxiously waiting for people to wear them for Halloween. Would you pick a funny mask or a scary mask for your costume? Why?

October 13

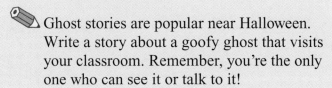 National School Lunch Week is in October. Tell about something you really enjoy about school lunches.

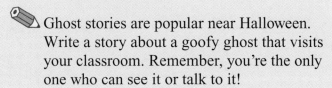 Ghost stories are popular near Halloween. Write a story about a goofy ghost that visits your classroom. Remember, you're the only one who can see it or talk to it!

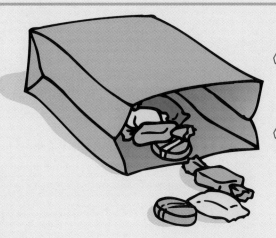

October 14

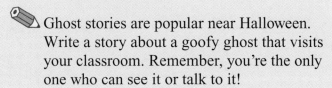 The second Wednesday in October is National Train Your Brain Day. Tell about something you wish you could train your brain to learn.

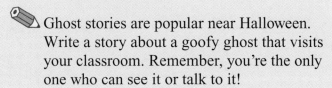 When you think of Halloween, you think of candy and more candy! Pretend you are a dentist. What would you tell your patients about the approaching holiday?

October 15

 Beware of grumps, gripes, and groans today—it's National Grouch Day! Write a funny story that could bring a smile to even the grumpiest of grouches.

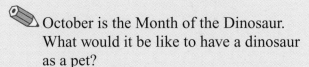 October is the Month of the Dinosaur. What would it be like to have a dinosaur as a pet?

October 16

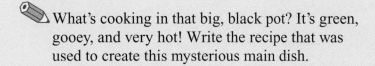 October 16 is Dictionary Day, celebrated in honor of Noah Webster's birthday. Look in the dictionary to learn the meanings of three words you didn't know. Write a different sentence using each of the new words.

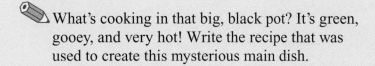 What's cooking in that big, black pot? It's green, gooey, and very hot! Write the recipe that was used to create this mysterious main dish.

October 17

 Leaves turn from green to an assortment of colors in the fall. Write a folktale describing an imaginary reason for why this happens.

Popular creatures to feature in October are bats and owls. These animals are *nocturnal,* or active at night. Write a story describing your way of life if you were to sleep all day and stay awake all night.

October 18

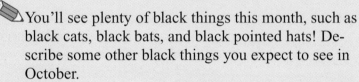 October is National Pizza Month. Create a pizza you think no one would eat! Describe the combination of ingredients that make it so unappetizing.

You'll see plenty of black things this month, such as black cats, black bats, and black pointed hats! Describe some other black things you expect to see in October.

October 19

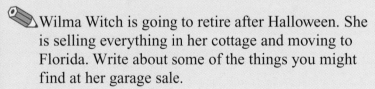 People could easily mistake a bat for a bird, but it is really a mammal—just like you! What would you do if you could be a bat for one night?

Wilma Witch is going to retire after Halloween. She is selling everything in her cottage and moving to Florida. Write about some of the things you might find at her garage sale.

October 20

 National Forest Products week is in October. Write about things in your house that are made from trees. Tell why these items are important.

You're invited to a Halloween dance where everyone is having fun doing the Bony Boogie, the Ghostly Gallop, and the Witches' Waltz! Write about your experience at this toe-tapping event!

October 21

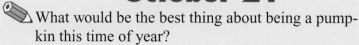
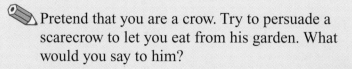

✎ What would be the best thing about being a pumpkin this time of year?

✎ Pretend that you are a crow. Try to persuade a scarecrow to let you eat from his garden. What would you say to him?

October 22

✎ Some people think the colorful autumn leaves are the prettiest sight of the year. Do you agree? Tell why or why not.

✎ Write a story titled "How the Jack-o'-Lantern Got Its Grin." Use your friends or family members as characters in the story.

October 23

✎ Imagine you are walking through piles of fallen leaves. Now imagine those leaves are fluffy feathers instead! Where do you think they came from?

✎ While walking home you see a creepy old house that you've never noticed before. What do you think you would see if you took a look inside the house?

October 24

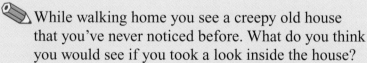

✎ Pretend you met a new friend who has never carved a pumpkin. Make a list of directions for turning a pumpkin into a jack-o'-lantern.

✎ October 24 is United Nations Day, honoring the organization that works for world peace. What can you do to make your playground a more peaceful place?

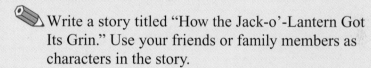

OCTOBER

October 25

The last seven days in October celebrate Peace, Friendship, and Goodwill Week. How can each of these things help make your classroom a happier place to be?

Halloween is coming soon! Describe a costume you would like to wear.

October 26

Author and illustrator Steven Kellogg has a birthday on October 26. Some of his many works include books in the Pinkerton series as well as the retelling of favorite tall tales. If you could write and illustrate your own book, what would it be about?

Today is Make a Difference Day. Who will notice that you made a positive difference in your community today? What will that person see you doing?

October 27

Would you rather be a scary jack-o'-lantern or a cuddly cat? Why?

Pumpkins, apples, and corn are some of the things that are harvested in the fall! Write a grocery store advertisement featuring some of the fruits and vegetables of the season.

October 28

Scarecrows are often seen standing guard over a growing crop. Imagine that a scarecrow could talk. What would he tell you about his day?

Popcorn, cornbread, and corn on the cob are just a few of the foods made from the corn plant. What is your favorite way to eat corn?

October 29

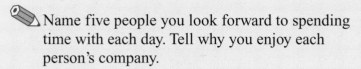 Make a list of words that rhyme with *trick*. Then make a list of words that rhyme with *treat*. Now use your lists to write a poem about Halloween.

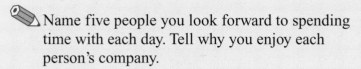 Name five people you look forward to spending time with each day. Tell why you enjoy each person's company.

October 30

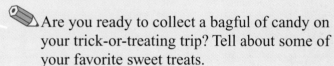 There's a whole cast of creepy characters ready to greet Halloween such as black bats, mean monsters, and spooky spiders! Write a scary story to set the holiday mood.

 Are you ready to collect a bagful of candy on your trick-or-treating trip? Tell about some of your favorite sweet treats.

October 31

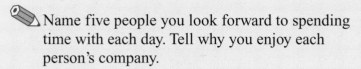 October 31 is National Magic Day. This celebration honors Harry Houdini, a famous magician who died on this day in 1926. Pretend that you are a magician. Write about one of the tricks you will perform during your act.

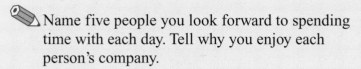 October 31 is Halloween! Write a list of safety rules for your fellow trick-or-treaters to follow.

November 1

✏️ National Authors' Day is November 1. Imagine you are a famous author. What will your next book be about? Who will the characters be?

✏️ Pretend you are a squirrel storing nuts for the winter. Write about where you will hide the nuts. What clues will help you remember where they are?

November 2

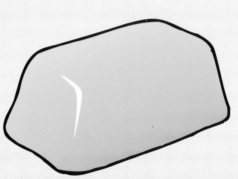

✏️ November is Aviation History Month, which celebrates air transportation of all kinds. Write about one way a person can travel in the air. Pretend it's your first flight in this type of aircraft. Describe your experience.

✏️ On November 2, 1889, South Dakota became the 40th state. Gold was discovered in South Dakota in 1874. It is still a large producer of gold. What would you do if you found gold while vacationing in this state?

November 3

✏️ November 3 is Sandwich Day in honor of the inventor of this handy meal, John Montague, Fourth Earl of Sandwich. Invent five new sandwiches and write a description of each.

✏️ Imagine that the colors of everything in nature got washed off. You're in charge of assigning new colors to things. What colors would you make the fall leaves? Describe how your surroundings look with the new colors in place.

November 4

✏️ November 4 is National Children's Goal-Setting Day. Write three goals that you would like to accomplish by the time this school year ends.

✏️ Pretend you are a goose. It's time to fly south from Canada for the winter. Plan your trip. Where will you rest along the way? What will be your final destination?

November 5

 Election Day is the first Tuesday of November. Write a list of at least five qualities that a leader should have. Number them in order of importance with number one being the most valuable trait.

Pretend you found a magical acorn under your oak tree. When you planted it, something mysterious happened. Describe what happened.

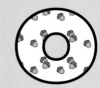

November 6

Pretend you are a cat. What are you thinking today?

You have just been invited to meet the governor of your state. What questions about your state would you want to ask him or her?

November 7

 World Communication Week is the first week of November. Select a country by looking at a world map or globe. What questions would you like to ask a child from that country? What would you tell him or her about your country?

The president of the United States has very important duties to perform and decisions to make. Write what you would do first if you were elected president.

November 8

Pursuit of Happiness Week is the second week of November. Make a list of things that make you happy. Tell why those things make you feel happy.

Think of an unusual way to use fallen leaves. Write about how you would convince people that this usage is important.

November 9

Yum! November is Peanut Butter Lovers' Month. Write an advertisement for the newspaper promoting a Peanut Butter Fan Club. Make sure to include the time, date, and place of your first meeting.

If you could climb into any book and become one of the characters, which book would you choose? Describe the character you would become.

November 10

November 10 is National Young Reader's Day. Why do you think it is important to learn to read?

Imagine that you are a turkey. What foods do you think should be on the Thanksgiving menu?

November 11

Pretend you are a tree. Several creatures are living with you. Name each of the creatures and describe what it is like to have each one as an occupant.

November 11 is Veterans Day. This is a day to pay tribute to all of the people who have served in the United States military. If you were in the military, what job would you like to have?

November 12

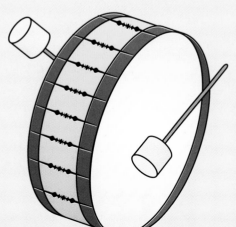

Drum roll, please...November is International Drum Month. There are many types of drums, such as snare drums, bass drums, kettledrums, and steel drums. What drum do you think you would like to play? Why?

The days are getting shorter as winter gets nearer. Why do you think this happens?

November 13

MRS. DAVIS DAY

✎ Think about the weekend ahead. Describe one thing you would like to do with your family that you've never tried before.

✎ It is your job to name this day in honor of a special person. For whom would you choose to name it and why?

November 14

✎ Many countries have yearly children's festivals. In India, for example, November 14 is Children's Day. What activities do you feel should take place on a day that honors children?

✎ What questions have you always wondered about, but don't know the answers to yet? Write four of them.

November 15

✎ If you could choose any day of the year to be your birthday, what day would it be? Why?

✎ National Geography Awareness Week is held the third week of November. Look at a map or globe and choose a country that you know little about. Write what you think it might be like to live there based on its location. Then read about the country in your library to see if your assumptions were right.

November 16

✎ The Great American Smokeout is the third Thursday of November. Write a commercial to encourage people to stop smoking—or to never start at all.

✎ Today is your day to invent journal topics. Write three journal prompts you would enjoy assigning to your classmates.

November 17

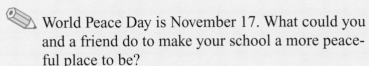

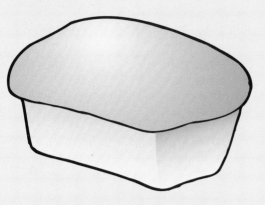

✎ November 17 is Homemade Bread Day. Write a recipe for your own newly invented flavor of bread.

✎ World Peace Day is November 17. What could you and a friend do to make your school a more peaceful place to be?

November 18

 Happy birthday, Mickey® Mouse! Mickey first appeared on November 18, 1928. Pretend you are Mickey Mouse and you are being interviewed on TV. Write how you would respond to questions such as "What's the best thing about living at Disney World®?" or "What is it like to be in a movie?"

✎ Fast-forward your life 20 years. What are you doing and where are you living?

November 19

 November 19 is Have a Bad Day Day. Imagine that your best friend is having a terrible day. What would you say or do to cheer him or her up?

✎ A cozy fire will warm up a chilly November evening. Pretend you are toasting marshmallows over the fire. Write about a new kind of toasted marshmallow treat you could invent other than s'mores.

November 20

 National Children's Book Week is the week before Thanksgiving. Write how you could make more time for reading.

✎ Imagine being a Native American who was invited to the Pilgrims' first Thanksgiving feast. What would you want to bring with you?

November 21

✏️ Bonjour! Hola! Ciao! These are all greetings you can use on November 21 to celebrate World Hello Day. Make a list of greetings you can say to your friends. Then set a goal to use your list to say hello to at least ten people today.

✏️ If you were going to create a beautiful piece of art, what tools would you use? Watercolors? Crayons? Clay? Write why you would choose the tools you did.

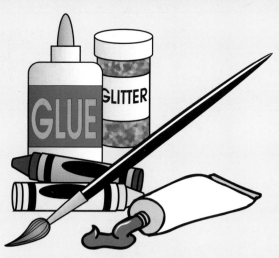

November 22

✏️ Imagine you're a turkey and you just found out you're on the Thanksgiving menu. What would you say to persuade people to serve something other than turkey for the Thanksgiving feast?

✏️ Describe how you think the Pilgrims and Native Americans cooked and baked the food for the first Thanksgiving feast.

November 23

✏️ Thanksgiving is a time to give thanks for all of the good things in your life. Write about five things for which you are grateful.

✏️ Imagine that your mom and dad let you plan and prepare a Thanksgiving feast based on your favorite foods. What would your family and friends be eating on Thanksgiving Day?

November 24

✏️ November 24 is "What Do You Love About America" Day. Imagine you're talking to someone who wants to move to America. Tell him or her what you love most about this country.

✏️ Imagine that you are a hibernating animal who has just settled in for your winter's rest. What are you dreaming about?

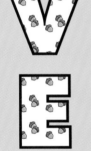

November 25

 Think back to Thanksgivings you have celebrated in the past. With whom do you usually spend the day? What do you do together when you're not eating?

 The week preceding the week with Thanksgiving is American Education Week. List several reasons you enjoy spending time at your school.

November 26

 National Game and Puzzle Week is the last week of November. Think about the games and puzzles you have at your house. Which are your favorites?

 You are about to pull the turkey wishbone with a member of your family. What is the wish you hope to come true?

November 27

 Write directions for making pumpkin pie.

Write directions for making pumpkin pie.

The Pilgrims traveled to America by ship and the ride was long and dangerous. Imagine if they had been able to choose a different form of transportation. What do you think they would have chosen instead of a ship? Why?

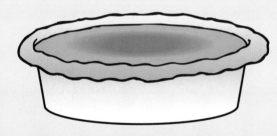

Dear Nigel,

November 28

Pretend you are a Pilgrim boy or girl. Write a letter to your friends in England describing your new home and life in America.

What have you done recently that would cause your classmates or your teacher to say "Thanks!" to *you?*

November 29

 In many parts of the country, where the weather's turning colder, the number of visitors to the zoo probably drops. Write a zoo animal's point of view about the change in temperature and the lower number of visitors.

 November 29, 1876, is the birthdate of Nellie Tayloe Ross. She was the first woman to become a United States governor. She was the governor of Wyoming. Write about something you would like to be the first one to do.

November 30

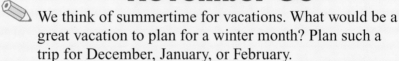 We think of summertime for vacations. What would be a great vacation to plan for a winter month? Plan such a trip for December, January, or February.

 Invent a superhero for a new comic strip that's about to be released. Describe his or her role in the community, and determine what his or her super powers will be.

December 1

December is the month for giving gifts. Write about a gift that you would like to give to a special person.

Mary Martin, the star of *Peter Pan,* was born on December 1, 1913. Imagine you could fly like Peter Pan. Where would you go? Whom would you take with you?

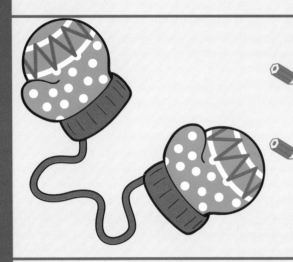

December 2

Pretend that you gave a friend a pair of mittens filled with goodies. What kinds of surprises would your friend find in the mittens?

Imagine that you are an evergreen tree. Describe what you see around you.

December 3

The game of bingo was first manufactured in December. Pretend that you are the Bingo World Champion. What would you want as your grand prize? Why?

The night sky is filled with twinkling stars. Imagine the stars make a picture in the sky. What do you see?

December 4

You just discovered that your new earmuffs are magical! Write about their special abilities.

Imagine that you are the runaway gingerbread man. Where would you run? Why?

December 5

It's Bathtub Party Day! On this day, people are encouraged to take long, relaxing baths. What would you take in the bathtub with you if you celebrated this special event?

Your hear jingle bells in the distance. Write about your adventure as you follow the sound of the bells.

December 6

Giving to charity is an important part of Hanukkah. What kinds of gifts would you donate to charity? Why?

Imagine that on your way to school you discover a house made of candy canes. What happens when you knock on the door?

December 7

Pretend you own a gigantic dreidel. Take a spin on the dreidel to anywhere in the world. Write about the place you visit.

Waiting for a special holiday is hard work. Waiting to open gifts is even harder! Write about the things you do to make your wait easier.

December 8

Imagine you just popped a batch of popcorn. When you removed the lid, you found a surprise inside the pot. Describe the surprise. How did it get there?

Write about your favorite holiday sounds.

DECEMBER

December 9

 December 9, 1886, is the birthdate of Clarence Birdseye. He developed a way to deep-freeze foods. Imagine you are a freezer. What foods would you like to hold?

 What is your favorite cookie? Describe how the cookie looks, smells, and tastes.

December 10

 Melvil Dewey, who invented a method for classifying library books, was born on December 10, 1851. Imagine that you are a librarian. Write about your interesting job.

 Pretend you have a new coat with lots of big pockets. What would you keep in the pockets?

December 11

 Write about your favorite place to shop. Why is it a special store?

 A delicious smell draws you into the kitchen. Describe what you find there.

December 12

 Poinsettia Day, December 12, is a day set aside for enjoying poinsettias. This interesting plant was first brought to the United States by Dr. Joel Roberts Poinsett. Pretend that you have just discovered an interesting new plant. Name and describe the plant.

 Think about someone who helps you. Write a letter to tell that person how much you appreciate his or her help.

December 13

✏️ The holiday season is filled with joyful noises. What kind of joyful noise will you make during this time? Why?

✏️ Imagine you are visiting Earth from a faraway star. What message would you bring to this planet?

December 14

✏️ The South Pole was discovered on December 14, 1911. Imagine that you are on a polar expedition team. Describe your adventures.

✏️ Pretend that you are a mouse in a busy department store. What do you see there?

December 15

✏️ Alexandre Eiffel, the man who designed the Eiffel Tower in Paris, was born on December 15, 1832. Imagine that you are an architect. Write about your most famous building.

✏️ Imagine you are a candle at your family's holiday celebration. Describe how you are used for this special event.

December 16

✏️ After playing in the snow all day, you go inside for a bowl of dinosaur noodle soup. While you eat, a real dinosaur suddenly appears at the table! Write about what happens next.

✏️ Imagine you have a talking ten dollar bill. What does it say to you?

DECEMBER

December 17

 Did you know that Wilbur and Orville Wright flew the first airplane on December 17, 1903? Imagine you were on that first flight. What was your adventure like?

 Pretend that you are a Christmas tree. Describe some of the decorations hanging from your branches.

December 18

 *The Nutcracker* ballet was first performed on December 18, 1892. Pretend you are a famous dancer. Write about what makes your dancing so special.

Which color do you like best, silver or gold? Why?

December 19

 Would you rather be a star or a candle during the holiday season? Why?

The first Christmas greeting from space was sent by satellite on December 19, 1958. Write a holiday greeting that you would like to send to the world.

December 20

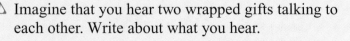 December is the birth month of several well-known poets. Write a poem about one of your favorite activities.

Imagine that you hear two wrapped gifts talking to each other. Write about what you hear.

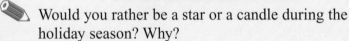

DECEMBER

December 21

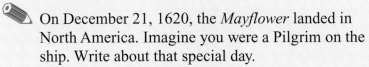

🖊 Holiday decorations are all around. Describe your favorite decorated place.

🖊 On December 21, 1620, the *Mayflower* landed in North America. Imagine you were a Pilgrim on the ship. Write about that special day.

December 22

🖊 Like a snowflake, you are special and unique. Write about the things that make you unique.

🖊 On December 22, 1956, Colo became the first gorilla to be born in a zoo. Pretend that your job is to take care of Colo. Describe a day with Colo.

December 23

🖊 Visit an elf's workshop in your imagination. Describe what you see there.

🖊 You are the first person to step out onto a fresh blanket of snow. Write about three things you will do in the snow.

December 24

🖊 Imagine you are a reindeer chosen for a special job. What is that job? Why were you chosen?

🖊 Write about your most wonderful holiday memory.

DECEMBER

December 25

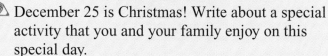

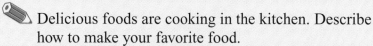
December 25 is Christmas! Write about a special activity that you and your family enjoy on this special day.

Delicious foods are cooking in the kitchen. Describe how to make your favorite food.

December 26

The first deaf teacher in America, Laurent Clerc, was born December 26, 1785. Write about some ways that you can communicate with a deaf person.

Kwanzaa begins on December 26. During this week-long celebration, Black Americans honor their families. Write about a family member that you respect.

December 27

December 27, 1822, is the birthdate of Louis Pasteur. He developed a way to kill harmful germs in milk. Describe your favorite food or drink made with milk.

Pretend that you followed a set of strange tracks in the snow. What did you discover at the end of the trail?

December 28

On December 28, 1869, a chewy treat called Blibber-Blubber was patented. Today, we call that treat bubble gum. Pretend you have just blown the world's largest bubble. What will happen next?

Imagine that a bird left you a note on the bird feeder. What did the note say?

December 29

✐ Take a pretend walk through some snowy woods. Write about the sights, sounds, and smells around you.

✐ It's time to give away some of your old toys to make room for your new ones. Where will you send the toys?

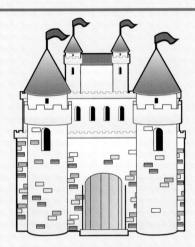

December 30

✐ Write about your favorite holiday photograph. What makes this picture so special?

✐ A candlelit path leads you to the door of a large, glittery castle. Describe what you see when you open the door.

December 31

✐ December 31 is Make Up Your Mind Day. Write about a time when you had to make an important choice.

✐ Tomorrow a new year will begin. What are you looking forward to in the new year?

January 1

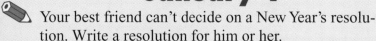

Your best friend can't decide on a New Year's resolution. Write a resolution for him or her.

Paul Revere, who is best remembered for his famous ride to warn the American people of the approaching British, was born on January 1. Describe what you think his journey may have been like.

January 2

You wake up on a cold morning and find that your bedroom has become an ice castle. Describe what you see and feel.

You have invented a way to make winter last all year. What are the advantages and disadvantages of having winter 365 days a year?

January 3

Imagine you are the lead dog in a dogsledding race. Write how you will help your team win the race.

What is your favorite winter activity? Why?

January 4

Jacob Grimm, co-author of *Grimm's Fairy Tales,* was born on January 4, 1785. Describe your favorite fairy-tale character.

Imagine that you migrate south every winter. Tell what you would pack in your suitcase and why.

January 5

✏️ The snowman in your front yard suddenly starts talking! What does he say to you?

✏️ Write about three ways you can help animals survive in the winter.

January 6

✏️ January is Oatmeal Month. Oatmeal is considered a healthy breakfast food. Write about the foods you eat for breakfast.

✏️ Imagine that you have the last bit of snow left on Earth. How will you keep it from melting?

January 7

✏️ If you had a magic sled that could take you either into the future or back in time, what time period would you visit and why?

✏️ Would you rather be an ice-skater or a hockey player? Why?

January 8

✏️ Imagine you are a snowflake. Write about your fall to the ground.

✏️ Compare winter in a northern state to winter in a southern state.

JANUARY

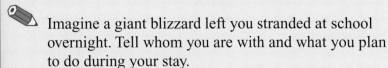

January 9

Pretend you are a disc jockey on your favorite radio station. Tell about and introduce your favorite song.

Imagine a giant blizzard left you stranded at school overnight. Tell whom you are with and what you plan to do during your stay.

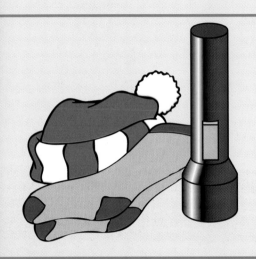

January 10

If you were a snowflake and could fall anywhere, where would you want to land and why?

What items would you pack in a winter survival kit? Why?

January 11

Pretend you are stranded on a floating iceberg. What would you do to pass the time?

If you lived in an area where snow didn't fall, what could you make "snowballs" out of?

January 12

What animals do you think enjoy winter weather the most?

A polar bear is protected from freezing temperatures by a thick layer of fat under its skin. What are some ways people stay warm in the winter?

January 13

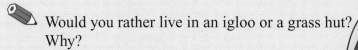 Which day do you like best, Monday or Friday? Describe three things you like about that day.

Would you rather live in an igloo or a grass hut? Why?

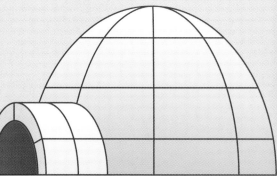

January 14

If you were a hibernating bear, what would you dream about?

National High-Tech Month is observed throughout the month of January to recognize the effect technology has on the way we live. Write about a simple task that you think could be made even easier through the use of technology.

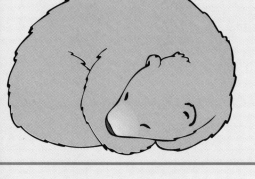

January 15

Think about the teachers who work in your school. Write what you think is the most difficult part of their job.

Imagine that you are a penguin. Write about the events that happen during a day in your life.

January 16

Celebrate National Nothing Day on January 16! Write how you would observe this day of nothingness.

Write about the very best places for a squirrel to find nuts.

January 17

Benjamin Franklin, who proved that lightning is electricity, was born on January 17, 1706. Write how your life would be different if there were no electricity.

Pretend your parents turned into snowpeople. How would your life change?

January 18

Pooh Day is January 18, the birthdate of the author A. A. Milne. Who is your favorite character from the Winnie the Pooh series? Why?

Imagine you received a magic sled as a gift. How will it help you?

January 19

Would you rather be a penguin or a polar bear? Why?

Jack Frost visited your house during the night. Describe the artwork he left on your windowpanes.

January 20

The third Monday in January is designated as the legal public holiday to honor Martin Luther King Jr. He is famous for his "I Have a Dream" speech. Write about your dream for the future of the people of the United States.

Pretend that you could hibernate through winter. How would you get ready for your long sleep?

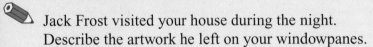
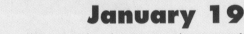

January 21

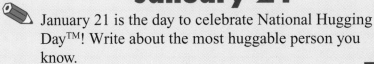 January 21 is the day to celebrate National Hugging Day™! Write about the most huggable person you know.

No two snowflakes are alike. In what ways are you different from the child who sits next to you?

January 22

 Answer Your Cat's Question Day is celebrated annually on January 22. What question do you think a cat might have? Write a response to its question.

Imagine there is no school today because too much snow fell during the night. Write about three activities you plan to do during the snow day.

January 23

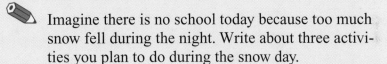 Universal Letter-Writing Week is celebrated in the month of January. If you could write a letter to anyone in the world, whom would you choose? Write what his or her response to your letter would be.

Would you rather live at the South Pole or the North Pole? Why?

January 24

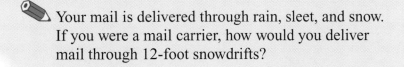 Imagine that you are part of a team that is building a snow fort. Write about the steps you would take to create it.

Your mail is delivered through rain, sleet, and snow. If you were a mail carrier, how would you deliver mail through 12-foot snowdrifts?

January 25

 The presidential inauguration is held in January every four years. If you were president of the United States, what changes would you like to make?

 National Soup Month is celebrated in the month of January. Imagine you are a chef who has just created a wonderful new soup. Write about your tasty new soup.

January 26

Some animals' fur changes to white in the winter to act as camouflage in the snow. If you could hide yourself, where would you hide and why?

What summer sport would be fun to play in the winter? How would the game change?

January 27

National Popcorn Day is held annually on Super Bowl® Sunday. Pretend your popcorn machine went berserk and now your house is overflowing with popcorn. What will you do?

The Super Bowl® is held annually on the last Sunday of January. Imagine you are the quarterback on one of the teams. Describe a play for making a touchdown.

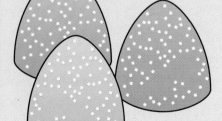

January 28

If all the raindrops were gumdrops, what would snowflakes be?

Plan a menu for a winter picnic.

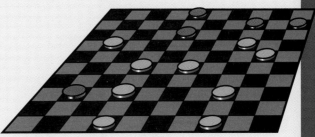

January 29

National Puzzle Day is celebrated on January 29. Write a description of your favorite puzzle or game.

In what ways are the clothes you wear in the winter different from the ones you wear in the summer?

January 30

In parts of the world, they experience days when the sun doesn't rise at all! Write what you would do for a week in continuous darkness.

The Chinese New Year celebration begins at sunset on the day of the second new moon following the winter solstice. Each new year bears the name of a designated animal. People born under a given animal's name are believed to have characteristics of that animal. Write about an animal you think you are like.

January 31

Scotch® tape was developed on January 31, 1928. Invent and describe a new use for Scotch tape.

What is your least favorite thing about winter? What could you do to make it better?

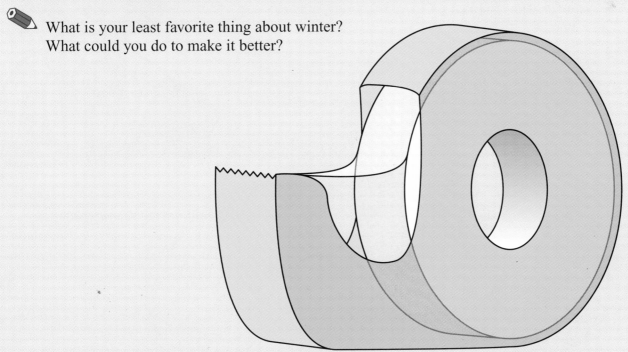

FEBRUARY

February 1

February is Black History Month. This time to recognize achievements and contributions by Black Americans was a weeklong celebration at one time. It has been the entire month of February since 1976. Who do you think should be honored in this month? What achievement or contribution is that person known for?

If there were a blizzard and you got snowed in at your house, what are five things that you would want to have with you? Explain why you chose each item.

February 2

Do you believe that a groundhog can predict the weather? Why or why not?

Imagine that your shadow came to life. Write about an adventure that the two of you had together.

February 3

Elizabeth Blackwell, the first woman doctor, was born on February 3, 1821. Is your doctor a man or a woman? Do you like to visit your doctor? Why or why not?

National Children's Dental Health Month is celebrated each year in February. If your teeth could talk, what advice would they give you about their care?

February 4

Charles Lindbergh, born on February 4, 1902, was the first person to fly alone, nonstop, over the Atlantic Ocean. What would you like to be the first person to do? Why?

Rosa Parks, a civil rights leader who refused to give up her seat on the bus, was born on February 4, 1913. Write about a time when you stood up for something you felt was right.

February 5

 Imagine that it snowed all night long. In the morning, snow covered all your windows and doors. What would you do?

 The Chinese New Year often falls in February. If you were asked to choose three goals for the year ahead, what would they be? Why?

February 6

 February 6 is also known as Pay-a-Compliment Day©. Whom would you like to give a compliment to and why?

 Pretend that you have a pair of magic skis. Where would you like them to take you?

February 7

 Laura Ingalls Wilder was born on February 7, 1867. If you were a pioneer, in what ways would your life be different than it is now?

 Explain the steps it takes to build a snowman. Begin your sentences with words like *first, next, then,* and *last.*

February 8

 What three words would you use to describe the month of February? Write three sentences about this month, using each of your words in a different sentence.

 The Celebration of Love Week is the second full week of February. The focus of this week is making the world a better place through love. In what ways could this be possible?

Thumpa Thumpa

FEBRUARY

February 9

 February is Responsible Pet Owner Month. What qualities make a good pet owner?

 What are some ways to show your family members that you love them?

February 10

 February can be a very cold month in many places. What do you think is the best way to stay warm?

 Look outside the window and observe the weather. How does a day like today make you feel?

February 11

 Thomas Edison was born on February 11, 1847. He is the inventor of many things, including the lightbulb. Describe how life would be different today if we did not have lightbulbs.

 Write about an invention you'd like to create. How would it help people?

February 12

 Abraham Lincoln, known as "Honest Abe," was born on February 12, 1809. Why do you think it's important to be honest?

 Lost Penny Day©, appropriately on Abraham Lincoln's birthday, is a chance to put saved pennies back into use. Where do you feel your pennies would best be used? Why?

February 13

 Plan ahead! February 14 is Read to Your Child Day. Write a letter to your parents persuading them to read a favorite story to you. Include reasons why this story is such a great read. Give the letter to your parents tomorrow morning—just in time for the special day.

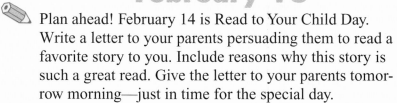

 The Daytona 500, a famous car race in Florida, is held every year in February. Imagine that you are a race car. How would you feel about traveling so fast?

February 14

 Imagine that Cupid just dropped an arrow in your classroom. How would you go about getting it back to him?

Random Acts of Kindness Week falls each year around Valentine's Day. Whom would you like to do something kind for and why?

February 15

Presidents' Day is celebrated each year on the third Monday in February. Imagine that you were just elected president. What would you do during your first day in office?

Describe some important safety rules to follow while ice skating.

February 16

National Pancake Week falls in the month of February. If you were planning the festivities for National Pancake Week in your school, what activities would you be sure to include?

 Describe how the perfect stack of pancakes looks and smells just before you take your first bite.

February 17

 What do you think the tooth fairy does with all of the teeth she collects?

What was the most interesting thing you learned in school during the past week? Why did it impress you so much?

February 18

 The planet Pluto was discovered on February 18, 1930. Write a story about an imaginary trip to Pluto.

Write a thank-you note to a friend for a special valentine he or she gave you.

February 19

 Imagine that you are a snowflake. Where would you like to fall?

 Create a new game that could be played during an indoor recess. Explain your new game and its rules.

February 20

 On February 20, 1962, John Glenn became the first American to orbit the earth. If you were John Glenn, how would you have felt during this adventure? Why?

 If you were able to choose the next president of the United States, whom would you choose and why?

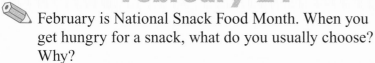

February 21

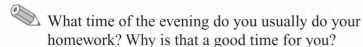

February is National Snack Food Month. When you get hungry for a snack, what do you usually choose? Why?

What time of the evening do you usually do your homework? Why is that a good time for you?

February 22

George Washington, our country's first president, was born on February 22, 1732. Do you think it would have been hard to be the first president of the United States? Why?

If you could be your favorite cartoon character for a day, whom would you choose to be and why?

February 23

Losing a tooth is exciting, but how do you think the tooth feels? Write about this event from a loose tooth's point of view.

What would life be like if there were no rules in your house? Would you feel differently about this than your parents?

February 24

Wilhelm Grimm was born on February 24, 1786. He was the younger of the two brothers known for publishing over 200 fairy tales. Which fairy-tale character is most like you?

What makes you feel scared?

February 25

As you stepped outside of your house this morning, you bumped into a sack. In it you found a small shovel, some jelly beans, and a bell. How could you use all of these things today?

Describe a time when you felt jealous.

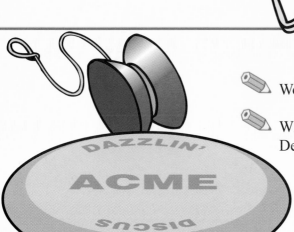

February 26

Would you rather be a yo-yo or a Frisbee®? Why?

Which animal would be the easiest pet to care for? Describe the care it would need.

February 27

February 27 is No Brainer Day. It's a day to relax and have fun! How would you spend a free day like this?

Have you ever felt sorry for someone? What caused you to feel that way?

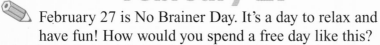

February 28

Describe your favorite memory of the past month. What made this event so memorable?

Think about the last time you celebrated a birthday. Was it yours, a friend's, or a family member's? What do you remember about that celebration?

February 29

✏️ Every four years there is a 29th day in February. How would you feel if your birthday was on February 29?

✏️ February has fewer days than any other month of the year. Why do you think that is?

February

			1	2	3	4
5	6	7	8	9	10	11
12	13	14	15	16	17	18
19	20	21	22	23	24	25
26	27	28				

March 1

 March 1 is National Pig Day! Wilbur, Babe, and Porky are three famous pigs who have had some marvelous adventures. Write your own story about an adventurous pig.

People say that March comes in like a lion and goes out like a lamb. Would you rather be a lion or a lamb? Why?

March 2

 March is National Nutrition Month. Pretend that the president is coming to dinner. Write a menu to show what you will serve. Make sure it's a balanced meal!

 Theodor Seuss Geisel, better known as Dr. Seuss, was born on March 2. He was known for his inventive illustrations and very funny verses. Draw a funny illustration; then write a rhyming verse to match your picture.

March 3

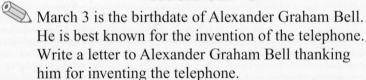

March 3 is the birthdate of Alexander Graham Bell. He is best known for the invention of the telephone. Write a letter to Alexander Graham Bell thanking him for inventing the telephone.

Happy I Want You to Be Happy Day! Write a note to someone special; tell about the person's special qualities.

March 4

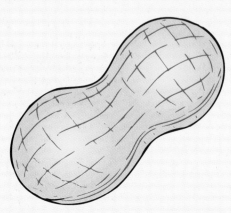

 March is National Peanut Month. Write about some important uses for peanuts.

 March is National Women's History Month. Research a famous woman. Write about her contributions to society.

March 5

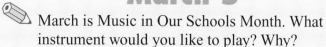 March is Music in Our Schools Month. What instrument would you like to play? Why?

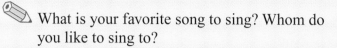 What is your favorite song to sing? Whom do you like to sing to?

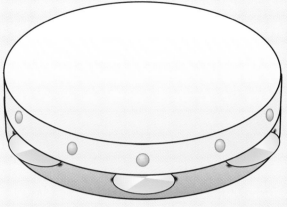

March 6

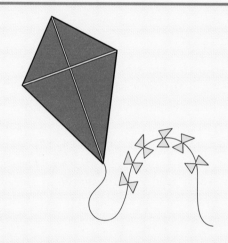

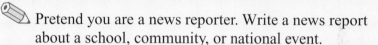 Imagine that you are a kite flying high in the sky at the end of a long string. Describe your feelings and your view as you soar above the ground.

 Pretend you are a news reporter. Write a news report about a school, community, or national event.

March 7

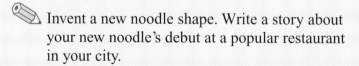 March is a big month for basketball. Pretend you are a coach wanting to start your own team. Who would you recruit to be on your team and why? Name your team and write about it.

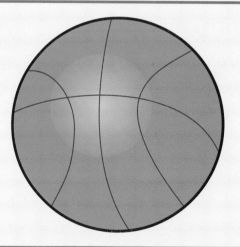

 Invent a new noodle shape. Write a story about your new noodle's debut at a popular restaurant in your city.

March 8

 Employee Appreciation Day is celebrated the second Friday in March. Write a note to an employee at your school to say thank you for the hard work he or she does.

What would you like to be when you grow up? Write a story about your future job.

March 9

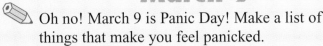

Oh no! March 9 is Panic Day! Make a list of things that make you feel panicked.

Are you tired of winter yet? By this time of year, many people are ready for winter to end. If you could travel somewhere warm and sunny, where would you go?

March 10

March 10 is the anniversary of the invention of the telephone. If you could call anyone in the world, whom would you call? What would you talk about? Write about your conversation.

Draw a picture of an invention that you would like to create. Write a story about your invention.

March 11

Pretend that you are a bird that is migrating back north after a long winter. Write a story about the journey from the bird's point of view.

Pretend that for a day you're in charge at home. Write about your day.

March 12

On March 12, The Girls Scouts of the USA celebrate their founding. This organization is enjoyed by girls nationwide. What club or organization do you belong to or would you like to join? Describe why you enjoy it or think you would enjoy it.

Imagine that you found a magic red shoe. Write a story about the strange, silly, or wonderful events that happen when you wear the red shoe.

March 13

 American suffragist Susan B. Anthony died on this date in 1906. Anthony was the first woman to have her likeness printed on a coin. What other woman is deserving of this honor? Why?

 Oh, how those March winds blow! Write a story about a very blustery day.

March 14

 The third week in March is National Poison Prevention Week. Draw a warning symbol that you would put on poisons to warn of their danger. Write why the symbol you created would help to protect people from the dangerous substance.

 Pretend that you have found a pot—but it's not filled with gold! Write a story about your pot. Be sure to tell what's inside!

March 15

 Potatoes are often used to make traditional Irish dishes. Write about four different ways that potatoes can be served.

 Write a story about a luck-filled day.

March 16

 Imagine that for one day everything around you turned green. Write a story about this day.

 Pick your favorite rainbow color. Write a poem or story about how this color makes you feel.

MARCH

March 17

 Happy St. Patrick's Day! On this day, everyone is a wee bit Irish. Write an adventure story about a mischievous, magical leprechaun.

Legend has it that all the snakes were driven out of Ireland at one time. Write a make-believe story explaining why there are no snakes in Ireland.

March 18

 Pretend that you are a daffodil that has just bloomed. Write a spring story from the flower's point of view.

 Imagine that you have just found a package of seeds. After you plant the seeds, something very silly happens. Write about the silly event.

March 19

 Imagine that you became a bird for a day. Write about what you might eat, do, or see.

Do you have a nickname? If so, how did you get the name? If not, what nickname would you give yourself and why?

March 20

 Hurrah! It's the first day of spring! Write a poem about the sights, sounds, and smells of spring.

 Spring's a time for playing outdoors, but sometimes rain puts a stop to that. What indoor activity would you do if it rained this Saturday?

March 21

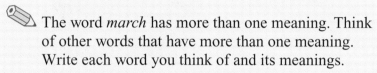
March 21 is Flower Day, a day to honor your state flower. Research to learn the name of your state flower. Write a folktale telling why you think this flower was selected to represent your state.

The word *march* has more than one meaning. Think of other words that have more than one meaning. Write each word you think of and its meanings.

March 22

Everyone needs one day a year to goof off, and there's no better day than International Goof-Off Day on March 22. Write a story about how you would spend a day like this.

On March 22, 1846, Randolph Caldecott was born. The Caldecott medal was named for him. This award is given to the illustrator of the year's most outstanding picture book. What book do you feel should win a Caldecott medal because of its awesome illustrations?

March 23

Maple sap is often drawn from trees during the month of March. The sap is then made into delicious maple syrup. Write a folktale about how maple syrup was first discovered.

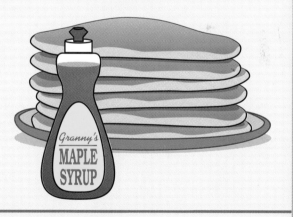

Imagine that you entered a time capsule and you are now living 50 years in the future. What is your school or home like in the future?

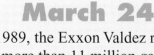

March 24

On March 24, 1989, the Exxon Valdez ran aground in Alaska spilling more than 11 million gallons of oil into Prince William Sound. Taking the point of view of one of the animals affected by the spill, write a story about this disastrous day.

Pretend that you are having a conversation with a bear that has just risen from his long winter's nap. Write a story about the conversation you and the bear might have.

March 25

 March is Youth Art Month. There are many kinds of art. Some forms include taking photographs, painting, making sculptures, and drawing. What is your favorite way to express your artistic ability?

 Imagine you suddenly spot a rainbow in the sky. How do you react?

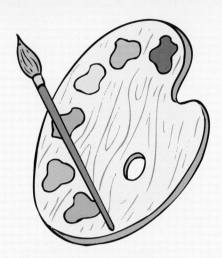

March 26

 March 26 is Make Up Your Own Holiday Day! Think of a name for your new holiday and decide how it will be celebrated. Write to tell about this new celebration.

 During the spring, pussy willows bloom. How do you think the pussy willow got its name?

March 27

 Pretend that an egg hatches, and something strange emerges from it. Write a story about the strange creature that has just hatched from the egg.

 Make up a silly new word for an everyday object. Write a story about the object using its new name. Be sure to include clues about the object's identity.

March 28

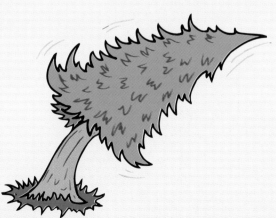

 If you had to eat only one kind of food for breakfast, lunch, and dinner for an entire week, what food would you choose? Why?

 Wind can be both helpful and harmful. Write about two ways the wind can be helpful; then describe two ways the wind can be harmful.

March 29

✏️ What would you rather do, climb to the top of a mountain or see the ocean floor in a submarine? Why?

✏️ Imagine a new friend moves in next door but you don't speak the same language. What are some things you could do together without having to communicate by talking?

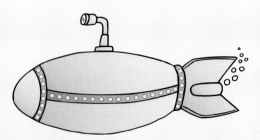

March 30

✏️ March 30 is the observance of Doctors' Day. Write a letter to your family's doctor thanking her for caring for you.

✏️ The Easter Bunny sent you a letter asking for your help this coming Easter. Write a letter back to the Easter Bunny giving him your decision.

March 31

✏️ On March 31, 1889, the Eiffel Tower in Paris opened. The tower, designed by Alexandre Gustave Eiffel, is one of the world's best-known landmarks. Design and draw a picture of your own national landmark; then write a story about your landmark. Include in the story what the landmark is made of and any special features it has.

✏️ List the names of some famous bunnies. Then write your own bunny adventure.

April 1

 Happy April Fools' Day! Write about the funniest April Fools' Day joke that has been played on you or a friend.

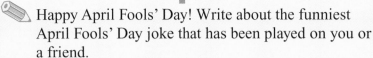 When it rains a lot, some people say that it's raining cats and dogs. How do you think this saying started?

April 2

 What do you like to do on a rainy day? Write about two things you could do *outdoors* on a rainy day.

 Hans Christian Andersen, author of more than 150 fairy tales, was born on April 2, 1805. Pretend you are a character in a fairy tale and have been granted three wishes. What would you wish and why?

April 3

 April is Mathematics Education Month. Write about some of the ways you and your family use math at home.

 Imagine that you could follow a rainbow to its end. Write about what you would see there.

April 4

 Would you rather be a rainbow or a raindrop? Why?

 Imagine that you are an umbrella. Write about your best feature.

April 5

Spring is the season for bunnies. In honor of these bouncy babies, write a rabbit tale about a big bunny family.

April is known for its wet weather. Pretend you are a weather forecaster. Describe the weather conditions you might have in the coming week.

April 6

Imagine that the Easter bunny decided he would not deliver eggs this year. Write a letter persuading him to change his mind about making his deliveries.

Old Man Winter doesn't want to leave even though it's April! Pretend that you are Spring trying to convince him to leave. Write about what you would say to him.

April 7

Imagine that while on an Easter egg hunt you find a very unusual egg. Describe the egg and tell what you will do with it.

World Health Day is observed on April 7. Write about three things you can do to keep yourself healthy.

April 8

April is Keep America Beautiful Month. Tell about some things you could do to keep our country looking its best.

Rainy weather can bring lots of puddles. Write a story involving a big puddle of water.

APRIL

April 9

Imagine that instead of an Easter bunny delivering eggs, a different type of animal took over the job. Write about a different animal delivering eggs on Easter.

Native Americans of the Southwestern United States perform a rain dance during the spring planting season. Would you like to participate in a rain dance? Why or why not?

April 10

"Rain, rain, go away. Come again another day." Write about two things you like and two things you dislike about rainy days.

Red is a color of the rainbow. Describe how the color red makes you feel.

April 11

Chicks, ducklings, and other baby birds are reminders that spring is the season for hatching! Write about some creatures that hatch from eggs.

How wet can you get? Write an adventure story about a rainy day when you got soaking wet.

April 12

ZAM! Zoo and Aquarium Month is celebrated in April. Imagine that you are an animal in the zoo or aquarium. Which animal would you prefer to be and why?

Children's author Beverly Cleary was born on April 12, 1916. Some of her stories include a motorcycle-riding mouse named Ralph, a friendly dog named Ribsy, and a lovably mischievous girl named Ramona. Tell about a character you think Ms. Cleary should put in her next book.

April 13

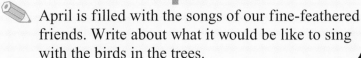
April is filled with the songs of our fine-feathered friends. Write about what it would be like to sing with the birds in the trees.

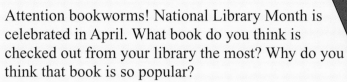
Attention bookworms! National Library Month is celebrated in April. What book do you think is checked out from your library the most? Why do you think that book is so popular?

April 14

A special baseball tradition of having the president throw the first ball of the season was started on April 14, 1910, by President William Taft. Pretend you could start a new tradition for the baseball season. Write about what you would do.

April is National Automobile Month. Describe the kind of car you would like to have when you are old enough to drive.

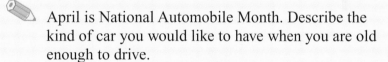

April 15

The eraser was invented on April 15, 1770. Write a legend explaining how you think this handy little item might have been created.

Think about a famous rabbit such as Peter Rabbit, Bugs Bunny®, or the Trix® rabbit. Write a description of the rabbit without writing its name. Have a class-mate guess which one you wrote about.

April 16

Gertrude Chandler Warner, author of The Boxcar Children® series, was born on April 16, 1890. The main characters in these stories once lived in an abandoned boxcar. What do you think it would be like to live in a boxcar?

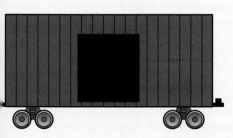
Bunnies hop, frogs jump, and toads bounce. How do you plan to leap into spring? Write about the first thing you like to do once the weather turns springlike.

APRIL

April 17

 April is National Poetry Month. Make a list of rhyming words. Then write a poem using words from your list.

 Thank You School Librarian Day is celebrated in April. If you were a librarian, which books would you recommend to readers? Describe your favorite two.

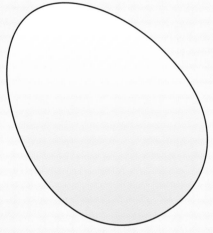

April 18

 Here's a puzzling question: Which came first, the chicken or the egg? Tell which one you think came first and explain your answer.

 Write a silly sentence for each letter in the word *April.* Here is an example for the letter *A:* Amy's amazing alligators ate apples and asparagus.

April 19

 Public Schools Week is celebrated in April. Write about the things you like best about your school day.

 What signs of spring have you noticed today? Write about these seasonal symbols.

April 20

 April is National Humor Month. In honor of this observance, write about a funny thing that has happened to you.

 Spring cleaning can be a big chore. Tell about some of the things you might see if you did some spring cleaning in your desk, locker, or bedroom closet.

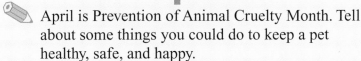

April 21

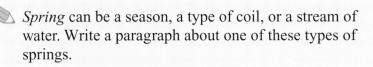 April is Prevention of Animal Cruelty Month. Tell about some things you could do to keep a pet healthy, safe, and happy.

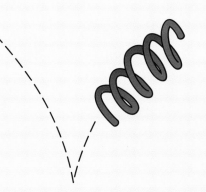 *Spring* can be a season, a type of coil, or a stream of water. Write a paragraph about one of these types of springs.

April 22

 Hello, planet Earth! April 22 is Earth Day, a time to remember to take care of our planet. Imagine that you are the earth. Write a letter telling people how to care for you.

April is filled with green—green grass, green leaves, and even little green bugs. Write about your favorite green things.

April 23

The first public school in the United States opened on April 23, 1635. How do you think schools have changed since that time?

National Arbor Day is a celebration for honoring trees. In most states, it is observed on the last Friday in April. Tell about some of the things in your class-room that were made from trees.

April 24

 What do you think "spring fever" is? Write about how you would feel if you had a case of spring fever.

How would you describe April? Is it as fluffy as a chick? As gentle as a lamb? Use comparisons to tell how you think of this month.

April 25

Now that spring is here, many animals will come out of hibernation. Imagine that you are an animal waking up after a long winter's nap. Describe your first day awake.

Rain can drizzle, drip, pour, pitter-patter, splash, and shower. Write a description of rain using these words and others.

April 26

John James Audubon, a scientist and artist who painted lifelike pictures of birds, was born on April 26, 1785. Try "painting" a picture of a bird using words. Use descriptive words to tell what the bird looks like.

Pretend you are a thermometer. Describe the changes you are feeling now that spring is in the air.

April 27

Write a job description for one of the following: mother, father, teacher, or coach.

April is National Lawn and Garden Month. If you were planting a garden, what kinds of seeds would you plant? Why?

April 28

Imagine having an unusual pet. What animal would it be? How would you care for it?

Use some or all of the letters in *raindrop* to make other words. After you have a list of ten or more words, write a story using words from your list.

April 29

✎ *Rainbow, raindrop, sunshine, springtime*—there are many compound words that tell about April. Write at least five sentences about April. Use a different compound word in each sentence.

✎ What sounds do you hear in April? Close your eyes and think about the sounds of the season. Write about the different sounds.

April 30

✎ April 30 is the last day of April. Tell about some of the things that have happened during this month.

✎ National Honesty Day is April 30. Explain what you think the saying "honesty is the best policy" means.

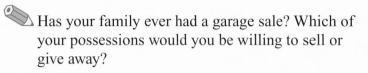

May 1

 May 1 is Mother Goose Day. What is your favorite Mother Goose rhyme? Why?

 Has your family ever had a garage sale? Which of your possessions would you be willing to sell or give away?

May 2

 An old saying goes, "April showers bring May flowers." Is this true where you live? Describe the plant life and flowers that you see out your window in springtime.

 May is National Hamburger Month. What do you like to eat on hamburgers, with hamburgers, or instead of hamburgers?

May 3

 Write about two ways you could get out of your house in an emergency such as a fire.

 The first U.S. medical school opened on May 3, 1765. If you were a doctor, what kind would you be and why?

May 4

 May 4 is National Weather Observer's Day. Describe the weather and how it will affect your plans for today.

 Imagine that you are in charge of the weather. Write about how you would change it.

May 5

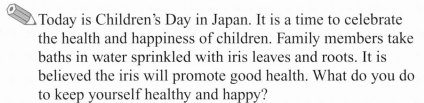
Today is Cinco de Mayo, a Mexican national holiday. Children often hit piñatas filled with candy and goodies. What types of treats would you want to find in a piñata?

Today is Children's Day in Japan. It is a time to celebrate the health and happiness of children. Family members take baths in water sprinkled with iris leaves and roots. It is believed the iris will promote good health. What do you do to keep yourself healthy and happy?

May 6

May is a good time to get outside. Describe two springtime activities you like to do outdoors.

You see a baseball, a football, and a beach ball waiting to be played with. Which do you choose? What will you do with it?

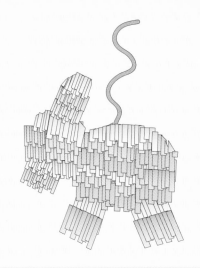

May 7

Johannes Brahms, born on May 7, 1833, was the composer of many beautiful musical works. One commonly recognized song is the Brahms Lullaby. Write about any special lullabies or traditions your parents share with you as you go to bed.

An expression says, "The grass is always greener on the other side of the fence." What do you think this saying means?

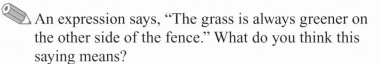

May 8

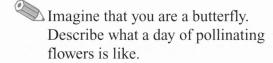
May is National Teaching and Joy Month. What is special about your teacher?

Imagine that you are a butterfly. Describe what a day of pollinating flowers is like.

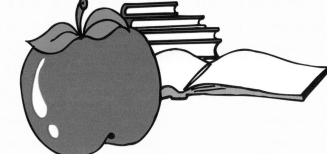

May 9

 Describe five things you could do backward today.

 Mother's Day is the second Sunday in May. What makes your mom so great?

Mom

May 10

 Why do you think people started the ritual of spring cleaning?

 The first full week of May is designated Be Kind to Animals Week®. What are some ways you are kind to animals?

May 11

 Imagine that you are a flower. What kind would you be and where would you want to grow?

If you could plant your own garden, what flowers and plants would you want to include?

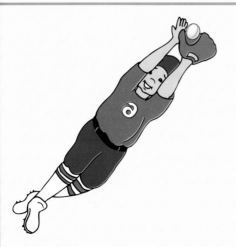

May 12

 Edward Lear, a famous writer of limericks, was born on May 12, 1812. Write your own limerick about springtime.

Spring is a great season for sports. Write about a sport you like to play or one that you like to watch.

May 13

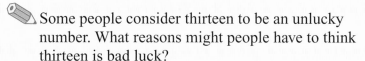 A week in May is dedicated to astronomy. If you could journey to outer space, whom would you bring with you?

 Some people consider thirteen to be an unlucky number. What reasons might people have to think thirteen is bad luck?

May 14

 Imagine that you are an ant at a picnic. What foods would you most enjoy?

 May is a month filled with blooming flowers and budding trees. Describe the other springtime sights you would see on a walk around your neighborhood.

May 15

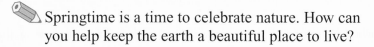 Lyman Frank Baum, author of *The Wonderful Wizard of Oz,* was born on May 15, 1856. If you could be a character from this story, whom would you be and why?

 Springtime is a time to celebrate nature. How can you help keep the earth a beautiful place to live?

May 16

 Nice weather in May encourages us to go outside. What chores or responsibilities do you have to complete before you can play?

 Imagine waking up on a spring morning, opening your window and hearing a bird bark, a cat chirp, and a dog meow! What would you do?

May 17

 May is the fifth month of the year. If you were able to decide the order of the months, how would you change them?

 Baseball season is up and running. If you worked at a ballpark, what job would you want and why?

May 18

 Today is International Museum Day. If you could design your own museum, what types of exhibits would you want to include?

 Take a look at the clouds outside today. Create a story about the pictures that you see in them.

May 19

 May is a great time to visit a zoo. What is your favorite animal to see and why?

 If you were an insect, which one would you want to be and why?

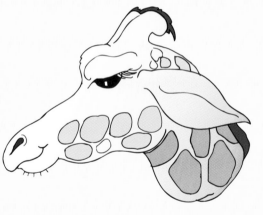

May 20

 Amelia Earhart flew solo across the Atlantic Ocean on May 20, 1932. Where would you travel if you could fly a plane by yourself?

 If you could build your own treehouse, how would it look? What would you be sure to include in your treehouse?

May 21

Pretend you are a mouse and you want a delicious-looking piece of cheese in a mousetrap. How will you get the cheese without getting caught?

List several words that rhyme with May. Then write a rhyming poem using words from your list.

May 22

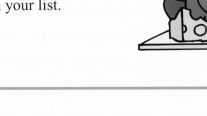

What do you enjoy most, in-line skating, bike riding, or skateboarding? Why?

If you could have any animal for a pet, which kind would you choose and why?

May 23

Imagine you are in charge of creating a classroom flag. Write about what it looks like and why you chose the colors and symbols that you did.

If you could travel down the stem of a flower and into the ground, what do you think you would find?

May 24

Butterfly is a compound word. List other compound words that remind you of spring. Now write a story using words from your list.

The sounds of birds chirping are one way we recognize spring is here. What other noises symbolize spring?

May 25

 May is named after Maia, the Roman goddess of spring and growth. If you could rename the month, what would you name it and why?

Imagine that you could bounce on a trampoline to the clouds. What would you see down below?

May 26

Sally Ride, the first American woman in space, was born on May 26, 1951. If you were to travel in a space shuttle today, what would you bring with you?

Imagine that you are a fluffy white dandelion and someone is about to blow on you. What you would say to that person?

May 27

  May is the month when many swimming pools open. If you are a swimmer, where is your favorite place to go for a swim? If you are unable to swim, do you think you'll want to learn this summer?

Imagine that mud pies could really be eaten. What flavors would you like them to be?

May 28

Memorial Day is the last Monday in May. Write about someone special that you will remember on Memorial Day.

You've outgrown your winter boots, mittens, and skis. What would you say in an advertisement to try to sell these winter items now that summer is nearly here?

May 29

 What is your favorite color? What things do you own that are your favorite color?

 School is coming to an end soon. What have you liked best about this year?

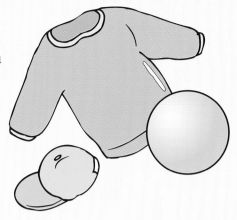

May 30

 The Lincoln Memorial was dedicated to Abraham Lincoln, our 16th president, on May 30, 1922. If he were still alive today, what questions would you ask him?

May is the time to get the barbecue grill ready. What is your favorite food cooked on the grill?

May 31

Have you ever been in a race? What kind of race was it? Did you win?

If April showers bring May flowers, what do May flowers bring?

JUNE

June 1

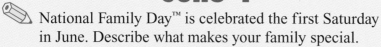
National Family Day™ is celebrated the first Saturday in June. Describe what makes your family special.

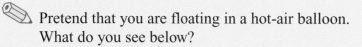
Pretend that you are floating in a hot-air balloon. What do you see below?

June 2

June is National Iced Tea Month. Would you rather cool off with a cold drink or a cold swim? Why?

If you could take a vacation anywhere in the world, where would you go? Why?

June 3

On June 3, 1851, the first baseball uniforms were introduced. If you could design an all-new uniform, what would it look like?

What do you like to do on a sunny day? Write about two of your favorite sunny day activities.

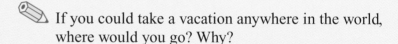

June 4

June Dairy Month is June 1–30. What would your day be like if you were a cow?

Some people say that the moon is made of cheese. If the sun were made of some type of food, what food would it be? Why?

June 5

 What are the best and worst things about drawing with sidewalk chalk?

 If you could invite anyone in the world to go on a picnic with you, who would it be? Why?

June 6

 National Patriots Month is celebrated from June 6 to July 4. What are some of the ways you can show that you're proud to be an American?

 Would you rather play miniature golf or go sailing? Why?

June 7

 If you could adopt a pet from an animal shelter, how would you decide which one to choose?

Is it more fun to play inside or outside in the summer? Why?

June 8

Ice cream was first advertised and sold in America on June 8, 1786. Invent a new kind of dessert. Write an advertisement convincing people to try it.

 Write at least three ways that dinner in a restaurant is different from a picnic in the park.

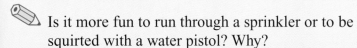
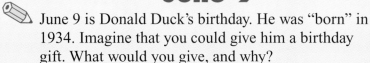

June 9

June 9 is Donald Duck's birthday. He was "born" in 1934. Imagine that you could give him a birthday gift. What would you give, and why?

Is it more fun to run through a sprinkler or to be squirted with a water pistol? Why?

June 10

Maurice Sendak was born on June 10, 1928. He has written many children's books, including *Where the Wild Things Are.* Pretend wild things came to your school. What might happen when they visit your classroom?

Does it feel better to cool off on a hot day or warm up on a cold day? Why?

June 11

June is Turkey Lovers' Month. Would you rather be a turkey or a penguin? Why?

Imagine that you built a rocket to visit the sun. Write about your rocket and tell about its special features.

June 12

Write about three things that you learned in school this year.

June is National Rose Month. Would you rather have a flower garden or a vegetable garden? Why?

June 13

 June is National Frozen Yogurt Month. Would you rather have frozen yogurt or a Popsicle®? Why?

 Graduation happens at the end of school. How is graduation also the beginning of something?

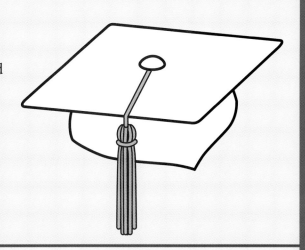

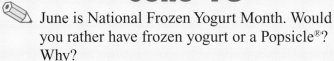

June 14

 June 14 is Flag Day. Why do you think we pledge allegiance to the flag?

 Would you rather wear shoes or go barefoot in the summer? Why?

June 15

 Father's Day is the third Sunday in June. Write about what makes your dad different from everyone else's.

 Imagine that you have caught a fish and it begins talking to you. Write about your conversation.

June 16

 What are three things you can do to keep learning while school is out?

 Pretend you are a hermit crab looking for a new shell. Write about the kind of shell you'd want to live in.

June 17

 June is National Fresh Fruit and Vegetable Month. Imagine that a watermelon could talk. What might it say to convince you not to eat it?

 If you could visit the beach, would you rather collect seashells or build a sand castle? Why?

June 18

 On June 18, 1983, Sally Ride became the first American woman in space. Imagine that you are the first American child in space. Write about what you see and do on your journey.

 Would you rather be an ant or a bee? Why?

June 19

 Garfield® the cat first appeared in the comics on June 19, 1978. If you could speak with Garfield, what would you talk about?

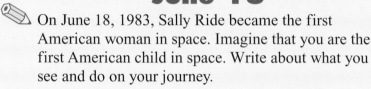 June 19 is National Juggling Day. Pretend you are a world-famous juggler. Write about the amazing things you can do.

June 20

 Write three ways that riding a bike and skating are alike.

 If you were going to send a message in a bottle, what would your message say?

June 21

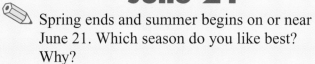

✎ Spring ends and summer begins on or near June 21. Which season do you like best? Why?

✎ The sunlight lasts longer in the summer. Write about three things you can do because the days are longer.

June 22

✎ If you were a firefly whose light wouldn't go on, how would you solve your problem?

✎ Summer is the season for thunderstorms. What are three ways you can tell a thunderstorm is on its way?

June 23

✎ People who own boats often name them. If you owned a sailboat, what would you call it? Why?

✎ Describe three ways that bears and people are alike.

June 24

✎ June is Fireworks Safety Month. Do you think it is safer to watch a fireworks display or a movie? Why?

✎ If your best friend went away for the summer, would you rather receive a postcard or a phone call? Why?

June 25

 Write about three ways you can show good sportsmanship when you play baseball.

 Sometimes hardworking people are called "busy bees." How do you think this saying started?

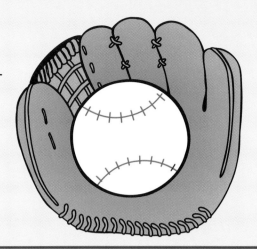

June 26

 Imagine you threw a Frisbee® into the air and it kept going until you could no longer see it. Write about where it might have landed and what happened to it there.

 Would you rather sleep outside in a tent or inside in a bed? Why?

June 27

 On June 27, 1859, a schoolteacher wrote the tune for "Happy Birthday to You." If you could spend your birthday any way you like, what would you do? Write about your special celebration.

 Is it more important for a house to have air conditioning in the summer or heat in the winter? Why?

June 28

 Imagine you found a magic rubber ball. What games could you play with it?

 If you had only one ticket at a carnival, would you rather buy a snack, play a game, or go on a ride? Why?

June 29

 In winter, children make snow pals and dress them in hats, scarves, and mittens. What kind of pal could you make in the summer, and how would you dress it?

 Pretend you're a baseball at a baseball game. What would you see?

June 30

 Imagine you could plan your own summer camp. Write about the activities you would plan for the campers.

 If you could travel across the country, would you rather ride in a plane, train, or car? Why?

July 1

✏️ July 1 is International Joke Day. Write about the funniest joke you've ever heard. Tell why it made you laugh.

✏️ On July 1, 1874, the first U.S. zoo opened in Philadelphia. If you could be any zoo animal, which one would you want to be? Why?

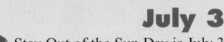

July 2

✏️ I Forgot Day is celebrated on the 183rd day each year. It is a day to recognize forgotten birthdays, anniversaries and other important events. How would you feel if someone forgot your birthday? What would you like them to do to make it up to you?

✏️ July is known as National Hot Dog Month. Pretend that you are a hot dog. Persuade someone *not* to eat you!

July 3

✏️ Stay Out of the Sun Day is July 3. The purpose of this day is to give your skin a rest from the sun's harmful rays. How would you keep yourself busy for an entire summer day without being in the sun?

✏️ Would you rather be in a parade or watch a parade? Write the reasons for your decision.

July 4

✏️ Describe how your family celebrates the Fourth of July.

✏️ How does it make you feel to watch a fireworks display?

July 5

July is recognized as National Baked Bean Month. What would happen if it rained baked beans for an entire day?

What would you do if your friend was playing with matches?

July 6

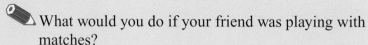

The first mid-summer Major League All-Star Baseball game was held on July 6, 1933. How would you choose the members of an all-star baseball team?

Imagine that you are a flower. What would you say to a person who was about to pick you?

July 7

Imagine you are taking a vacation this summer. List the five most important items to pack in your suitcase. Explain why those items are so important.

If you could live anywhere in the world for the entire summer, where would you choose? Why?

July 8

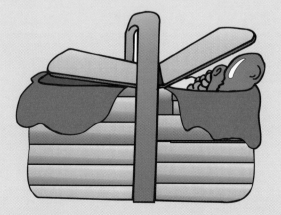

Describe the ideal picnic spot. What makes this place so perfect?

What smell most reminds you of summertime? Why?

July 9

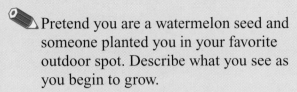 Make a list of the top ten things that you like to do when you are not at school.

Pretend you are a watermelon seed and someone planted you in your favorite outdoor spot. Describe what you see as you begin to grow.

July 10

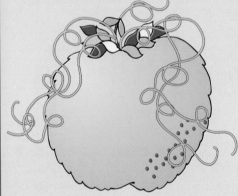

What are some ways to protect your skin from the sun's rays?

Invent a new type of fruit. What does it look like? What does it taste like?

July 11

 Write a review of a favorite book that would make someone want to read it.

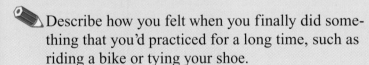 Describe how you felt when you finally did something that you'd practiced for a long time, such as riding a bike or tying your shoe.

July 12

When it gets very hot outside, what are some of your favorite ways to cool down?

If you were taking a vacation, would you rather travel by boat or by train? Why?

July 13

Do you think bees are helpful or harmful? Describe your reasons for feeling the way you do.

You jumped into your neighborhood swimming pool and discovered it was magical. What happened to you when you hit the water?

July 14

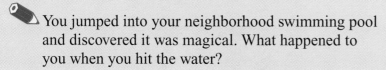

What is your favorite summertime memory of all? Why?

Do you prefer playing in the snow or playing in the sand? Why?

July 15

Rembrandt, a famous painter, was born on July 15, 1606. Would you rather paint a picture or a house?

Would you rather eat a tomato or a potato? Why?

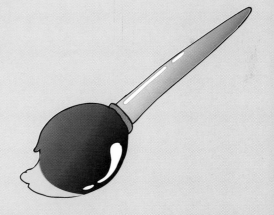

July 16

Imagine that you are an ant. Which picnic food would you most like to find? Why?

Do you think it would be fun to work at a zoo? What would be the best or worst part about the job?

July 17

✏️ Would you rather be the pilot or the passenger on an airplane? Why?

✏️ Create a new game that could be played in a swimming pool. Describe the game and its rules.

July 18

✏️ Imagine you just built a huge sand castle. Describe it.

✏️ Many people go camping in the summer. How do you feel about camping?

July 19

✏️ Write a folktale titled "How the Firefly Got His Light."

✏️ A Popsicle® is a popular summertime snack. Do you think that it would also make a good wintertime snack? Why or why not?

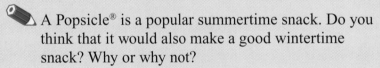

July 20

✏️ Space Week is held each year in July. It commemorates the July 20, 1969, landing on the moon by U.S. astronauts Neil Armstrong and Eugene Aldrin Jr. What do you think are important qualities for an astronaut to have?

✏️ How do you think the practice of roasting marshmallows began?

July 21

✏ Write a list of safety rules for people to follow when they're at the swimming pool.

✏ If you could change your name, what would you change it to? Why?

Pool Rules
1. No running
2. No pushing
3. No food in pool

July 22

✏ Which insect is your least favorite? Describe how it looks and explain why you don't like it.

✏ Write a story about an adventure in space. Include some of your friends as characters in your story.

July 23

✏ Imagine you have set up a lemonade stand on a busy street corner. What would you say to persuade someone to buy a glass of lemonade from you?

✏ If you went for a long bicycle ride and got lost, what would you do?

July 24

✏ Amelia Earhart, the first woman to fly solo across the Atlantic Ocean, was born on July 24, 1898. Would it be exciting or scary to fly that far alone?

✏ You're at the circus. You have to choose between cotton candy and popcorn for a snack. Which will you pick? Why?

Popcorn

July 25

✏ Do you prefer to go to your neighborhood pool or to the beach? Why?

✏ Your mom lets you choose a vegetable for dinner. Would you pick green beans or carrots? Why?

July 26

✏ If anyone in the world could move in next door to you, whom would you like it to be?

✏ How is your neighborhood different in the summer from in the winter?

July 27

✏ Look at the clouds in the sky. What do they remind you of today?

✏ Many people take their dogs for walks in the summer. Do you think that a dog should always be on a leash when its owner takes it out for a walk?

July 28

✏ What are the best and worst things about eating watermelon?

✏ If you could make a wish upon a star, what would you wish for?

J U L Y

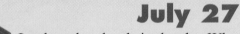

July 29

✏️ What do you most enjoy doing when you're at a park?

✏️ Would you rather be a turtle or a rabbit? Why?

July 30

✏️ Henry Ford, creator of the Model T Ford, was born on July 30, 1863. Imagine that you are a car. What kind of car would you be? Describe your features.

✏️ Paperback books were first introduced on July 30, 1935. If you were a book, would you rather be a hardcover or paperback? Why?

July 31

✏️ If you were a frog, would you prefer to live in the wild or as a pet? Why?

✏️ Make a list of the things that you would still like to do before the summer is over. Why is each thing important to you?

My August Journal

by _____

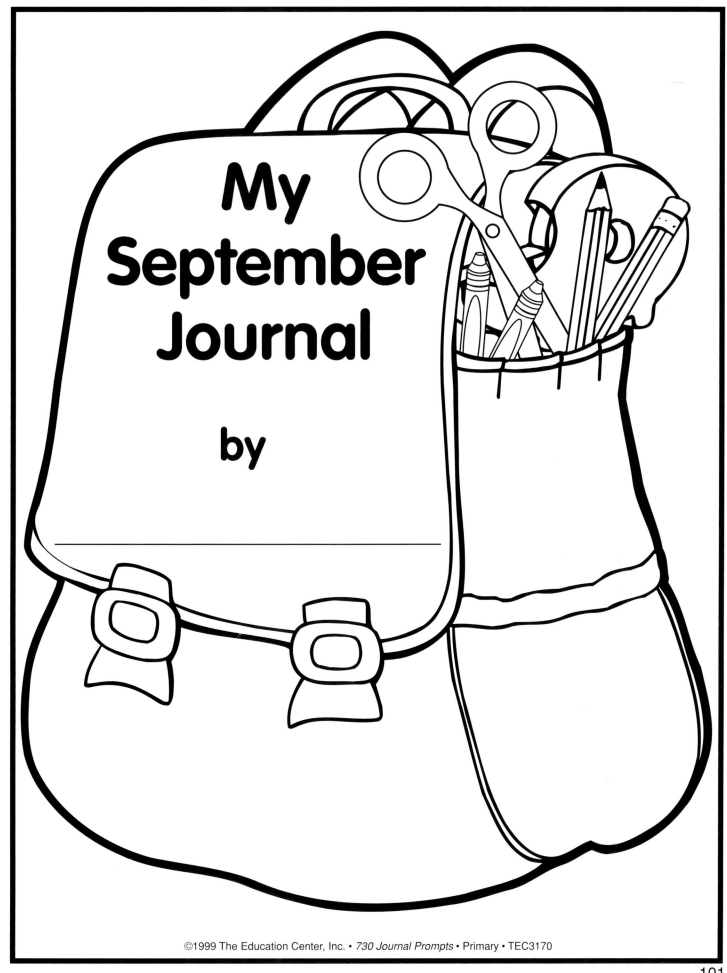

My
September
Journal

by

_____

My October Journal

by

_____

My November Journal

by _____

My December Journal

by _____

My
January
Journal

by

_____

My February Journal

by _____

My March Journal

by _____

My
April Journal

by _____

My May Journal

by _____

My
June
Journal

by _____

My
July
Journal

by _____